MIRACLE TO CRACKLE

Pebbles we all say NO!

Sundeep koul

BookLeaf
Publishing

India | USA | UK

Dedication

Once upon a time jack and Jill went up the hill to fetch a pale of water. Jack fell down and broke his crown and Jill came tumbling after. Seriously the stories which can make or break a situation is not important when one identifies; who were Jack and Jill? ; Why did they went up the hill? Why only one pale of water ?; who pushed the jack?; why did Jill tumbled down? What happened to the pale of water?. There must be a reason for their adventure and a great learning for all the toddlers who grew with it singing and rhyming the same. **Poems are stories by themselves.**

For me as well one inspiration leads to the other. One poem illuminates the other. This pint of ART which is 'MIRACLE' is duly dedicated to my **prime GURUS** in life. **"For my dad, who taught me the love of stories, and my mom, who cherished them."**

"PRANA KOUL my dear 'MEIJ' and MAKHAN LAL KOUL my dear 'MOUL'

Each idea which becomes an inspiration to fight or flight comes from the early learnings and their impact is visible in your phycological and physiological behaviors barring Deeping reflections on your self and your world which surrounds you. Book dedications are a wonderful way to remember someone or something integral to you or your journey for writing. They're meaningful to you as an author, since you've been inspired and moved by them, and they're meaningful to the subject you making an impact over.

Preface

"Miracles happen to those who believe in them." – This powerful quote comes from Bernard Berenson, an American art historian.

Close your eyes and take a deep breathe, let us take a journey in values of importance and read them through the poetic verses. Each line has one direct meaning and a story by itself. This journey of expressing my knowledge has come from my **48 years** of experience i have gone through cycles of RESET-TRANSFORM-SUSTAIN. No life is easy and no being is painless, however the core 21 values which I am making a poetic dive into will reflect and touch upon your lives too.

Each poetic story is a factory of beliefs, environments, collaborations, self awareness and motivation for making ones life meaningful as we tread it on the segment of life BD. 'B' being the **Birth** and 'D' being the **Death**. It is the Alphabet '**C**' between the **B** and **D**, the **choices** one make to <u>set, sort and shine</u> your **SELF** and other adjoining lives too.

READ , **READ**, and **READ** it , unless the "**DEAR**" SELF in you gets invoked, and that will be the success of the MIRACLE for sure you believe in the most.

- **"ME CRACKLE" for MIRACLE is the objective**

- **"KNOW YOUR MIGHT"** , do not say 'NO' TO YOUR MIGHT

Acknowledgements

The inspiration for inking down the wired thoughts does not come naturally unless one starts to believe in making a humble attempt to weave the story of life living through the values one can have. I literally acknowledge " **THE THIRSTY CROW STORY**" which brings the core concept of **MIRACLE** for everyone.

Once upon a time, there lived a crow. One summer day, the crow felt thirsty and began to look for some water. It flew over the fields but couldn't find. It felt exhausted and it was about to give up. Then it saw a jug near a farm. It quickly landed down there to check whether there was any water. It looked inside the jug. There was some water. It wanted to drink but couldn't reach the water because of jug's narrow neck. It tried to push it down, but it was too heavy. It thought a while. Then it looked around and saw small stones. It picked the stones up one by one and threw them inside the jug. Thus, the water level rose up enough and it quenched the thirst thanks to its clever plan.

MORAL: We are all such birds in life and there are values as pebbles all around us. The desire and the real outcome only come through if we give the life a strong push to come up. Such pebbles would always be around us to help it quench better and provide a value to the system as well. WHAT WE GIVE IS WHAT WE GET and what we GET is WHAT GETS PERPETUATED around too. Be the thirsty crow and identify your pebbles for MIRACLE to set in your lives.

FIRST IS THE LEAP OF FAITH

Close your eyes and let us take a journey of values,
miracle it promises with deep lovely hues.
slaying this belief is never gone to give you merits,
staying with it is the game that always fits.
LEAP OF FAITH or PEEL OF FAITH is the choice one
can take, promises galore and energy sure to make.
Let us rumble in the city of life one has we think, it is
never a stone carving or a contract to ink.

Sometimes you call it faith and other times the belief, it
demands attention like ocean's own coral reef.
There are scenarios where you would be put to test, it
could just be a stir with high energy and no good rest.
It does not come naturally the way you are born, it
resounds close by with high pitch horn.
it is fed by others and gets nourished on its own, the life
makes you dance like a silly looking clown.

Seen numerous trying to give it a full throttle try ,Smiles
they anticipate ; makes one to sob and cry.
Can there be a template to copy and paste, can there be a
way simple with no time waste.
Each story that gets created and played in full, is a mix
of tries and cries varying in push and pull.
Yet each one of us takes the faith to leap, backed by
failures and blessings to sow and reap.

Take a step back and see your approach , does one
needs a guide or a life coach.
You could be doing it all well, however no matter what;
it grows into a curly hell.
Something must be fine tuned to set it right, that may be
the hope in close sight.
Breathing is a process we feel cannot be learned, nothing
stays same, it can very well be churned

Hover around your supporting structure and cast, absurd
is to claim the broken stale past.
Is there someone who is peeling the faith, is there
someone who has put; you on machine lathe.
Is there a treachery brewing around , is there a game
being played with mute and no sound.
Are you being lead to unfollow your faith to leap, are
you being pushed not to cherish your own actual reap.

It is to differentiate between the real and fake, it is all
about one decision you always have to make.
There will be resistance for re-peeling to heal, all it takes
one leap of faith to feel.
Action and reaction will always stand there, you will
need to play the life always fair.
let your fears fail and they structure cool , leap of faith is
all what makes life a joyous pool.

It is all about knowing when one need to peel, it is all
about knowing when it gets worse to feel.
Speaking about it is a way to abort, never think it is "the
end" you have more ways to sort.
Self care is the need of time to kick start the belief, be
your own tribe and stay as your own chief.
FAITH, FAITH and FAITH is the POWER one got,
MIRACLE it is; let it not go unsort.

SECOND IS THE KINDNESS

There are people who are kind, there are people who
stare it with eyes blind
There is no dearth of commitment i guess, for sure the
more you do , the more it feels less.
You are kind is the feedback you want, do you work for
it, for sure I believe not
Kindness does come running and straight from heart, it
has its own virtue that is why it beats fast.

Let us deep dive and see where do you stand, do you
have the ground for the flying **KINDNESS** to land.
Let us begin with the placement and charter for you , it
is the behavior that will never be over due
When was the last time you were kind for self as it
begins, when was the time you were for it all
scales and fins
Wise and elders always say charity begins at home,
living in reality needs working be it here or Rome.

Neither it needs planning nor it needs a book, it starts
within , just requires a clean slate look.
It will surely come and pass by with sign, it definitely
shows up whether it is yours or mine.
The inclination to commit for help is profound, a small
act is needed till you find its ground.
One who gives the fruit of kindness gets joy in leaps,
happiness is the key and blessings it reaps

The fruit of kindness is perpetual as it is never a waste,
no matter what the condition is; it always has taste.
It gives one the hope of help to cherish, glow and bloom
it goes with no signs to perish.
Why does one say it is a fruit and not a seed, this is
the food of though t I want to feed.
Let us call the fruit of kindness as the seed to groom ,
giving it the nourishment like magical broom.

Yes you head me right the miracle of seeding , you heard
me right the miracle of feeding.
What one give is always what one receives as gain, love
begets love and so would reflect the word pain.
Harder it gets as harder you stay away from fact,
tougher it stays as resistive you stay away to act.
What is keeping you away not to give it a try, life stays
not forever in midst of happiness and cry.

You might be thinking how smartly one gives it a kiss,
aptly thinking what will happen; if I give it a miss.
World is filled with generosity and many noble souls,
what will happen if there are few holes
No one bothers it to be seen as always perfect, gosh!
why do we look at excuses and bother to select.
We do overthink it only for some baseless issues, work
on it over and over with no connected fuse

Take a pledge and be the noble soul, **MIRACLE** is one
pint away if one fills the empty hole
You need not be an expert in the game , you need not be
doing it just for the fame
Step in as takes to cover the entire ground, a pledge for
sure will make it a try round
Seeding the Kindness is the best miracle one can grow,
bet it ! you can and you will reap it as you sow.

THIRD IS THE TOUCH OF LOVE

The easy thing one takes granted in life is **LOVE**, is it so
simple to understand , if yes; tell me how?
They all say it is in the air if you have its sign , they all
say it glows around and make things fine.
you cannot hide it as it smells in air , you cannot contain
it as it rallies and stays fair.
there are stories to make when it catches its beat, there
are tales to make when it kept clean and neat.

The genesis of this miracle is visible only when it
blooms, it fills your heart and beats in all four rooms.
Does this virtue has its onw story to sell , may be love
itself has some feeling to share and tell.
Let us begin the journey by thinking love as person that
lives, it is a cup of nectar that only gives.
It is simple and never blinds itself in bonding , it is open
book and has verses full of fonding.

When it takes the form it is a baby new born, cherish-
able and curious with no prickly thorn.
It flies high and looks for its steps next, it dances high
thinks what and how to text.
It looks around for help and and a possible host, never it
would have thought for getting roast.
It thinks all are alike and tries best to be with all, damn!
this is where humpty dumpty had the great fall.

The more it tries to get support and link, the more it
finds itself going down the sink.
It tries it s best to stay with foot right, wants to get
attention with no possible fight
This is the realization for its growth, when all along the
way it finds all lies and full loathe.
It gets more murkier as it tries to be the story, hate
becomes the present and past becomes gory

Then it distils and thinks about the connections it made,
only mother tops the list rest all becomes fade
Comes then the rhymes and stories the father
gave, followed by chimes and games the siblings pave.
Friends and pals makes it on the list too, they become
sunshine and give smiles like 'Vinnie the pooh'.
Few strangers make the entry as wild card, for sure love
begets love; it is simple yet so hard.

The love as being is a miracle by form, it remains still ;
whether fire or deadly storm.
By its virtue, it the giver in character, neither fake nor a
paid looking actor.
It gets caught in woes of blame, question yourself for
you being lousy and lame
You gave it a rosy picture to live in reels, stress takes
form and really hurt all as it feels

COMM 'on gear up and take care of this friend, life is
short with all crazy and curly looking bend.
You have got one life to try it bloom for sure, care is the
demand so stay real and pure
Faking it can make you popular in a box , makin it real
can save you from being a lifeless fox
Cunningness is the not the value it teaches, it stays deep
inside to all frontiers it reaches

MIRACLE of love is a trick to practice must, love is
love and not just mere lust.
Develop it and see where did you fail, practice hard act
quick for real fairy tale
It all starts and become stars one day, while the sun
shines one must make hay
It is the only ray of hope for faith and kindness, learn
and practice; don't make it yourself a mess.

FOURTH IS PERSEVRANCE

A spider in my back yard having one dream , hanging
down by one strand ; getting ready to beam.
Every time trying his best to roll the body up, pulling
it fast to achieve his dreamy cup
The more he pushes the harder it gets, the more he
rushes the far he sets.
Every time he gives the best shot and rushes again,
sadness and apathy I see, as he achieves no gain.

He looks at me and winks with a smile , thinking wait
and watch I am not running out of mile
Neither a movie nor a drama to praise, it is pure courage
with flavor full of craze.
Spider is my name and trying not is not in my game.
I have learned it good and truly in the past, one who
tries, tries and tries can surely long last

With pushes after pushes he reaches at the top, away
from the floor and away from the mop.

Holding tight the roof he clinked with a sigh, crazy
courage pulls you low and pushes you high.
Now reaching the top he spins the home, takes rest like
in sauna and relaxing bubble foam.
Does it mean the end of struggle for him, does it mean
end of sadness in cellular rim

The story seems so familiar and simple to read, spider
kept trying and was ready to lead.
Setting an example is so common in wild, situations
would never be easy and mild.
There would be challenges you would wish to go, there
would be upsets were you will only listen NO.
Growing in maturity is the thing life teaches, it is design
by nature as the the lesson of persistence reaches

One needs to be consistent to stay truthful, one needs to
be consistent not to be broken full
Failures are like season which comes and goes, life is
your own picture be ready with happy pose
Persistence pays you installments of joy and progress,
flighting away harms more and warns less
There are no signals and highways express, success is
never sure if you tread your path less

Rowing your boat is the task always in hand, persistence
will help your flight and fight to land.

Whining is the not the way to web the platter, winning
comes by practice now and by not acting later
Spider gave me a lesson; for sure he is right, skill and
will are two virtues let us not argue and fight.
You are responsible to take your control in hand,
persistence and consistency will help you fly and safe
land

FIFTH IS TO EMPTY THE FILTH

One can call it filth and one can call it trash, if you hold
it more you are sure to crash.
It is modernized as holder or recycle bin, whether
you are plastic or paper it sounds tin.
It makes you diseased and gives you rash, diced you
become ; sometimes potato mash.
More you discover it quickly the more you earn,
MIRACLE is all yours if you want to learn.

What tops the bin you need to keep the eyes open wide,
what fills the tin , you don't need to hide
Is it the EGO which you massage all day, or is the
phrase 'you go' which rages the dry hay.
Are you listening to only yourself making others mute,
you are all tabla and no sweet flute.
Gosh! the above trash will make you live aloof , it will be
a complete building with luxury; but no roof.

Love is the nectar which one should keep must, don't
make it just a game of pure play lust.
It puts a dent on this sweet car, it gives out a millage but
not drives far.
It colludes the basic nature of giving in love, it pollutes
the basic necessity dull for now
Give a try to put a control on it, it is not easy if you
think to walk but only just sit.

Attachment is also one such virtue not to side, it is not
easy practice one can leave to ride.
It leads to expectations for giving and taking, it could
be the love or lust in making.
One needs to identify the threshold to scale less,
detachment is the only answer to stay out of mess.
You can keep in touch and not touching each other, you
can keep close and not nosing each other

Anger is something sure to forget and skip, it keeps
combing your ego and love to rip.
It heats up and burns your chamber of art, it beats up
and beats the heart apart.
Brings down the shutter for the relationships, breaks the
lovely bonds like crunchy chips.
You can save yourself from this danger of fire, burns you
down and your house more as it goes higher.

One such ailment is named as greed, it swells more and
grows gross without a seed.
Gets nourished by ego; anger and lust, it looks spick and
shiny with deep hidden rust.
it can make you lose the **MIRACLE** quick, it can make
you lousy meaty and diseased; so sick.
The greed takes you and make you older and tire, it sells
you out or put you on showcase hire.

The filth of all as stated above is more damaging as it
seems.
The trash of all as dressed above is relentless as it beams.
The virtue of putting it down the drain is all in your
might
wrong is wrong and having it by your side is never going
to be right.

SIXTH TO SHOW AND LIVE COURAGE

Coming so far was your belief in the MIRACLE you got,
it needs one to have courage and energy a lot.
You will be asked to go narrow and wide sometimes, you
will be asked to stay low and high at times
You would have sobbed in your silos for sure, looking for
breaking walls and easy ways to cure.
The days would have longed with full of wait, one
becomes the victim and sometimes bait.

Remember lion and mouse; the jungle story book, king
has the beat and throne to cherish and look.
Ultimate was his life and his ruled state, lots of food and
family with no worry on the plate
He was eager to kill and pounce on things , he was eager
to fill and bounce in hunting rings.
Cannot draw myself for comparison with king , cannot
stage my prowess like his hunting sling.

There was a mouse living beside his place, he was
running with with freedom of lace.
The king caught him live while he napped , furious he
goes as mouse was cluelessly snapped.
The moment of truth was about to happen for end, he
was getting ready to to be eaten in mouth bend.
If you are imagining to be a mouse in life here, this is the
moment of truth ; so be fair.

With a pint of courage one must raise the toast, it was
just that mouse who pleaded for freedom the most.
I could be of some help tomorrow , i could be of some
favor you can borrow.
King laughed at him for being small and said, you are
sensibly small for hunger and help to fed.
Go away and and don't show me your face, you are free
to enjoy your freedom race.

In reality there are similarities to be drawn from lion and
mouse
There would be context where someone else or you can
be in such hard house.
Sow the kindness as the lion unknowingly is setting for
story to go
Show the courage like the mouse for freedom is all what
one needs to know.

The same lion was one day caught by hunter and was
sad, there was no one to help with a feel bad
Here came the mouse as he was apt and skilled, cutting
the net as helper role he smilingly filled.
When was the last time you were on this page, when
was the last time you showed up courage.
The story has the same relevance and is still to act,
fighting or flighting is the basic need in fact.

Courage for self and rage for others is not in balance , it
is not for sure the sign of healthy valence.
You can be the master and help others as well, all it takes
the MIRACLE to swell.
Courage is the behavior one definitely needs at heart,
learning and practicing is sure to be in kart.
Let us all be the lion or mouse sometime, living
with freedom , dignity and courage to rhyme

SEVENTH IS TO BE THE BEACON

Looking for an idol in life is all one need, we keep
wondering till it pops out for a right feed.
The adventure of finding that moment becomes
sometimes live, there is a world out there with full
beehive.
One gets stinged and pain of swellings, one get lost in
the sea , ocean or land dwellings
There we need a proper indicator or a light of some sort,
why does one worry and unknowingly get caught

Treading the journey from being kind to fearless, it all
needs one potion ;that is you i guess.
If you fail; you still create a story for all, you show the
world where not to fall.
You show them how to win and put hefty fight, you
show them the hope for that glow and light
You are spoken and given reference for, you bring that
sweetness with tinge of sour.

Beating the dead horse is completely futile, there is lot to
learn from the X-file.
For sure majority never references it, they think who has
time to dig the lousy pit.
They might not see you as help again, for them without
handwork ; they want to gain
Excuses are worthless to ponder being lame, in the end
they are the ones who are sure to blame.

There goes a story of a shepherd boy who cries foul,
every time he goes to forest gives the false howl
Villagers would run to the woods with axe and rock, to
drive away the creepy and wild hungry fox
Disrupted by the laugh the shepherd boy does, they
would return in dismay for the false call he buzz.
They never tried to mend him for the way he was on, it
was surely a practice to begone.

This prank was getting popular every time they hear,
running way up down the woods for visible fear.
one day the boy tried one more howl , as there was a real
fox behind him and running fowl
villagers set relaxed this time and acted cool, they never
wanted to be looked as fool
Boom goes the catch this time as shepherd runs to live, a
false alert prank land him in tears few.

There is so much to see and so much to hear, never be
the shepherd boy to end in tear.
alerting for false is not set fine, you could be the next in
wild for dine
it breaks the trust and breaks the ship, it fills the story
with wrong sad and chip
Gosh! it is never late we learn from mistake, beacon for
right is only left to make.

The stormy sea and ocean has such numerous ships, we
act reckless till the emergency chips
we start shouting in despair and pain, we start asking for
help in deep sorrow to be utterly vain.
Never it strikes us that it could be someone closer to us,
never it strikes that we cold have reduced fuss
Simplicity is the name sometime one hear, it is all up to
us to see the beacon ;why fear?

Raise your wall and hit the ocean shore, each one of us
can become the BEACON as core.
we could be the ones who can show the ships the way,
give them warning and hope of light ray.
Bet me if you have lived the MIRACLE till date, you are
sure to change your coming fate.
**Being an ICON is a BEACON for sure, Being an idol is a
blessing so pure.**

EIGHTH IS TO MOTIVATE

Coming so far was magical for us , reading so hard was
without any word cuss!
All along the way we see values galore, all along the way
we see people joining so more.
There are occasions and events which will put you to
test, all what you need is good clean rest.
Moving in game and shoving you to glory is great, acting
NOW and acting right now ;it is never late

Thought it sound like a long wait in the end, don't stop!
as there is lot to look over the bend.
It is potion which comes with no expiry date, it depends
on you; never to take it as agreed fate
There is lot to learn and share when you travel, life is
smooth; though sometimes it will have gravel.
It surely will go in rocks and boulders in time, wait is the
key; sing it with positive rhyme.

There are resources who will pull you up, they will
provide you with energy and comfort cup.

They will storm in and help you anyway, Life does give
friendly beats; need attention to pay.
You can be your help every time all time and again,
Seasons are bound to have showers and ugly rain.
It needs some courage to practice as i know, be your own
light; nevertheless it will surely glow.

Bringing up your brightness is your own small bit, get
up; shrug it; shake it; give it a reply fit.
It is fearful and surely cease to exist, it can neither be a
story nor can remain in a gist.
Motivation is a cup with no daring weight, remember
good deeds to give ;it is never too late.
You can be a taste for the world around, you can be the
waste and stay on the ground.

Lift yourself up and lit your dream, sit over the action till
you see the light beam.
Key to motivation lies with no locked door, it only needs
you to work precisely more
You could see it handy around your support, it travel by
ship in sea and river by boat.
It finds its ways all by hard-work to put up, stay no still
as there is world to say What' sup!

It takes hardship to find the diamond so right , it takes
hard to wind that coil so tight!

The twinkle it shows blows one's mind, the recoiling of
the spring takes some grind
If you stop because you were lazy, if you stop the world
will not call you still crazy.
Self realization is what it takes to share, even the lava
which gets got solidifies pays its fare.

People will wait and weight it in their lazy thought, it is
life and so is living; don't me the clumsy bot.
World is full of AI coming soon Oh! dear, sip your tea of
motivation and play it neat n fair.
Sea can be rough and ocean can be tight, important is
not to loose your silly old sight
Rivers are crazy and the lakes is quiet, water surely finds
its way for it has got its MIGHT

MIRACLE MIRACLE MIRACLE! what a way for
MOTIVATION to CRACKLE.
MAGIC MAGIC MAGIC ! what a way for MOTIVATION
to set flick
LIGHT OF HOPE, it shows in the END
as MORE YOU GO LIFE offers a beautiful BEND

NINE WITH DEDICATION

The word has many forms centered to a locus, it really
needs a fully dedicated and formalized focus.
You might think , it has always been around , you might
think , it has always kept you on the ground.
Worked well in the past and remained a buddy great,
revived you always and never kept you wait.
Well the journey needs one to take a right stand , it
builds your house of MIRACLE and your flight to land.

There are seven alphabets which make the word
DEDICATE, you miss one of those surely lock one's fate.
The first alphabet 'D' being the DELICATE so good,
teaches us to remain careful and carefree as it would.
One must be sure which end to go and strike a side , as it
is all about being truthfully wide.
Delicate is also to bring out the intrinsic taste, surprising
the surrounding with no time to waste

The second one 'E' should bring the EMPATHY on
platter, knowing the present and nothing to be later.

It helps us to Strike the accord of belief to be in, it
teaches us to stay for love and care with no sin.
It grows more only when you know each other, try to
control it ; can change your weather.
There is no scale which can let you know why you are,
there is no measurement to keep it close or far.

The third alphabet 'D' once again tells you to DESIGN, it
will be stormy and sometimes weather so fine.
You need to meticulously set time for your plan, you
need to set your ways to keep up healthy clan.
Being delicate and empathetic is must to make start,
designing through INTEGRITY will surely long last
'I' the integrity is virtue very important to dedicate, it is
never electronically the OR but is the AND gate.

Fifth being the 'C' is all about you CARE , it is always
within your reach to be fair.
You need to be in to seek its attire, you need to be in to
meek its satire.
Getting it from others is always we think , be the
initiator for the CARE to wink.
All it wants to live in you and others around, make it
a habit for self and others to sound.

The sixth in line is the Alphabet 'A' ,
ACKNOWLEDGEMENT it mirrors with care in its bay.

It needs to show and stay in healthy stance, slow and
fast it can be; it is there to dance.
You never ask for it ; it shows up right, it brings along
the happy showers light.
Makes one believe the worth it provides, open ness
totality with no taking sides.

The seventh star 'T' is the TRUST we get as treat, it gives
the word DEDICATE ;the required seat.
The practice of belief gets sorted here, MIRACLE it gives
with a feat of Cheer.
It multiplies more and gets added so high, divides the
burden and subtracts the lie.
It gives the peace the piece you require, it takes the piece
as the peace your fire.

Last one in the DEDICATE is the alphabet 'E' so big,
neither it bears a mask nor it flaunts a wig.
Yes the word is EARTH the planet where one live, it is
something which only knows to give.
We can imbibe the quality it shows, it is universally life
so big with no defined foes
DEDICATE for sure is a vaseful BOOK, MIRACLE need
to be followed; not just for a poetic look.

TENTH IS TO BE HONEST

The element of honesty is always on the fence, a shot for
each moment; so important hence.
Without this core element one ceases to exist,
without this the care and empathy is out of list.
It does justify why dedication is needed to be in count,
without which honesty has no mount.
It feeds all the desired values one needs to show, it leads
all the desired values one needs to row.

Think of love to be without this grain, to be honest it will
always be cloudy with tearful rain.
There will deceit all in the air with foxes flying, there
will be hate and only hate with heart burns lying.
Trust will never be plying and living happily without , it
will be a well ; a dry deadly pit to shout.
People will be thirsty and ready to stab back, trust will
loose its seat for honesty in lack.

Kindness comes straight right from heart, it will be dry
and cry without honesty on chart.

It will be a movie which fails without been made, as
kindness would be shallow with color fade
Motivation will find its way down the drain, as the dish
would be tasteless without honesty as grain.
It will be more a reel and not a real scene, no matter who
pumps it with energy keen.

Courage will be a child who would never see teen, it will
be a life with no progression seen.
Honesty not being around will hit hard in this game ,
people will forget the courage for being lame.
The only element which we need to give away as filth
will remain with us
Gosh! the world will be full of mess , ego and infectious
fuss.

There will be anger and danger living inside, no honesty
means treachery will just lurk and glide
We will live in the world of lies and sorrow, as there
would honestly be no happiness to borrow.
Justice will be just a lip service for no support, a sure
shot flop show discussion in court.
The peace will get a hit on face and kick on the back, all
the values will just stay in books and rack.

HONESTY is a core for any value to be successful and
beaming with joy

By not keeping it on your side we are heading towards a
deadly scenic ploy.
Remember your identity is also based on the honesty
when journey had begun
TAKE it! and don't FAKE it, not making it impossible to
RUN.

ELEVEN TO BE RESPECTFUL

When one stands together by side of each, it is for sure
the MIRACLE of eleven to teach.
It is never the thing which which is demanded to get, it
is to be earned which grows more as you net.
The MIRACLE of respect comes the way you grow, it
does come shooting without an arrow and a bow.
There would be stories for all of us to reflect, it is quiet a
world and lot of connections in fact.

It begins with RESP as in responsibility to fleet , ends
with FULL to make ends meet.
It is the quality one needs to look and pick more, it is a
definite reality not just a folk lore.
It amuses your beat and makes you work hard, it fills
your mind with absolute happy card.
It makes one listen to the inner being one is at ease , if
you never show up it will soon make exit and cease.

Do you think you can invoke this pebble of thought,
giving more to it than the more you sought.
It dies for sure if you think the return is fast , it lies on
the sick bed with no shadows to cast.
There will be a ghost so empty and dull, there will be a
host with nothing to sell.
It will demand attention the way it slicks, it punches less
than the more it kicks.

The flower has the respect for the twig who folds it, the
leaf give the same to the branch who holds it.
Branch on the ground stays proud due to stem in guild ,
stem stays strong for there are roots to build.
It is the soil which brings nourishment to the root to
grow, it is the soil who gets it from the garden row.
The garden gets it all from the sun as it lit, the sun gives
photons for leaves to sow energy fit.

There is cycle of life in the nature all around , there are
all giving ;with sharing leaps and bound.
The question is who teaches them this aspect, they are
fixed and still they cherish this respect.
With no words of wishes in return and no hand shake, it
is all real and sounds not at all fake.
They share the common element of life in punch, they
stay together from brunch to crunch.

Just ponder when was the last time you receive it , or
when was the last time you deceive it.
If you give it a slip you are bound to get a slap, working
for it makes one to get a sure clap.
Giving it is the shear joy one gets to fill, it is like going
down the lovely green hill.
Respect is the MIRACLE which give a happy sip, it builds
you in blocks and beats till you RIP.

TWELVE IS WONDER OF CARING

It is a double treat when one is gifted with wonder and
care, twelve is the count if you are here
You have reached so far for the magic you felt ,
unleashing the eleven stars on your journey belt
Reading the verses have given you a story to frame,
connecting them in your lives is not so lame.
It is a scenario which gets untouched never, what is lost
and why is lost is a question forever.

Does it mean we get lost in the past , with sadness and
despair not to cast?
Or may be a great memory to cherish, which helps to
gain memento before we perish.
When I say we CARE let us be careful, let us not fear but
still be fearful.
Living in memories of past which we cannot wipe , why
do we help the casting shadows to ripe.

Does one should be careful for the future to come, past
for sure needs a kick on the bum
Does it make a difference if we only think, who cares if
the present has got nothing to link.
Dreaming about it and nothing concrete to act, here one
needs to show the care in fact.
Not being the fan of the past or the coming time, present
is the wonder where one bets the dime.

Remembering those big hands when you were small,
carrying you everywhere so that you don't fall.
Helping hands to take those small steps and walk, trying
to give all care when you were toddler talk.
Sky had no limits when they were for you, seasons alike
with happiness undue.
Colors of joy everywhere with full on games, how soon
one can forget that care and those names.

The life moves and you get friends and foes, you show
care for buddies as the time flies and goes.
There was care for maturity as you lived, there was dare
around you sometime shrived.
Those moments your buddy was all your beat, those
were the times you were given the comfy seat.
The times changes as you show no care to friends, I
wonder it was not anticipated as it really ends.

There were siblings and cousins which you would flaunt
so big , naughty and funny games to dig.
The care for each other was never slow, there was all
deck buckled up with music and glow.
Not sure if the growing does all the trick, same sets of
people we believe was love; starts to prick.
We start taking our own sides as we are right, GOSH! it
is the time when one begins to fight.

Showing the care for self is must and a definite need, it is
the most basic thing one forgets to heed.
Life gives these wonders and will test you out, it will be
a harder and sometime softer bout.
Having the ability of giving this care to all, holding the
hand when someone is about to fall.
That is the level of MIRACLE one needs to show, care for
self and care of others to know.

THIRTEEN IS THE LESSON FOR PATIENCE

why does it sound like patient when one fickles, why
does one becomes impatient when life tickles?
I am PATIENT or IMPATIENT both reflect the same, it is
after all a pebble which one needs for game.
The number 13 is unlucky as the lesson is so tough, if
you slip on this ; the life will surely be rough.
Taking the guard for the this PEBBLE is vital, it is in
your might! that why MIRACLE is the title.

Imagine you start running before you crawl, humpty
dumpty for sure; will have miserable fall.
One starts jumping without the run you take, the more
you jump the harder your back will ache.
No says the bird when he tries to fly, predators will keep
a look and will pounce to sly.
There is no shame in accepting if one jumps the gun
before, impatience is the the devil ;you store.

The question is; does one get time to learn for being
calm, or does one get to see an apple on coconut palm.
We can be imaginative and can think all good, sure it
was true if there was no cobra; having vicious hood.
Reality always plays and bites around, imagination has
no true sky and no strong ground.
Let us try to fine tune the pebble by staying kind,
patience is something which is not tough to find.

Think patience as a person who wants to make a mark,
consider you just met him while jogging in a park.
He looks gloomy and strikes a pose sad, was he really
wavering or faking his shape bad.
I was told by MIRACLE of my might to be caring,
kindness was another pebble to remain in sharing.
I went close to patience and asked what is the issue , you
are sobbing; do you need a tissue?

He laughed and smiled with a grin on face, he sprung
back with his answer full of sugary lace.
I may be sad because you left me here, I may be sad since
I see you in deep fear.
I see you running around when you need to rest, I see
you always putting yourself to test.
you are not bad at all as you keep it inside, emotions are
meaningful if you learn to abide.

Why do you hurry when you can stay pause , why do
you worry when you can find the cause.
Count from one to ten and then react, it is just one
technique simple in fact.
You will learn it by practice if you try, that can make my
eyes not to cry.
You can see me jogging along with you , as for my advice
there are takers few.

So that was the revelation for me in the park, it was my
own self patience left in dark.
It was me who was sobbing and sad , it was me who was
running so bad.
It was me who was trying to find the windings , it was
me who was bothered to check the findings.
Gosh! it sounds the pebble I found, what goes out really
comes in sound ;all around

Remember one LESSON for the patience it teaches, it
needs to be opened up till inward it reaches.
You can stay kind and humble to add it in your jug, yes it
does need sometime a healthy warm snug.
Controlling the FILTH as in chapter five, you can very
well love it to keep the kindness alive.
PAT on the BACK is you all require at will, this is how
MIRACLE rises up the clouds over the hill.

FOURTEEN TO BE HUMBLE

Generosity is the virtue for being HUMBLE , This is the
time for pebble to jumble.
Staying low and keeping kindness in kitty, one needs to
know and use them to be witty.
Don't get filth to take over and break you here, let the
generosity as pebble on your side play it fair.
If you know that you are in control and keeping it tight,
BOSS! for sure you are absolutely right.

HUMAN and HUMBLE has HUM of sound, it tells one to
stay kind and soulfully on ground.
It is somehow closer in relation to be kind, it is somehow
closer for being easy to find.
Though being humane we sometime fake it, being
humane we some time make it.
Humility is the pebble that brings peace profound, it
gives kindness the wings with trust in bound.

Consider generosity as a library of books, full of
knowledge and kindness as it looks.
It is kept in a grand big house of wax , nice it looks as
shine it gives always max.
The wax house holding the library is so nice with detail ,
heat as element can bring it down without fail.
We try to keep this house tidy and clean, it should serve
purpose of generosity i mean.

The books are dusted and building is vacuumed, we
barely get it raged or we keep it off getting fumed.
There is no chance of error as if it catches fire, the flames
would melt down the structure as wax goes higher.
We keep it guarded and try our best, we keep it shiny as
Humility makes it a haven and nest.
Did you had the second thought if the wax building is
you, hate and heat can bring it down with no clue.

Library is the mind you have got in the head, it carries
the books humble with generosity to fed
Books are the opportunities where you can show your
might, keeping them clean and tidy is the only fight.
You can dust off the mind and keep clean content,
humbleness is the way not keeping ego on rent.
That is the fire which can keep the mind warm, it will
surely melt down the house with kindness to harm.

Keeping it shinning and keeping just the ego away, can
make your house safe and sound in a way.
No heating will generate no melting for books,
humbleness will stay in corners and nooks
You will cherish the fruit of its might , as it will keep the
pole star twinkling all night.
The way shown by it will always be rightful, for sure it
will ensure you to remain sightful.

The miracle of might always says one must be generous
for self and others in line.
It is the magic one needs to have for self and to have
place for others to be fine.
There would be distractions and flitty pebbles around.
There will be criticism and shouts mute and sometime
sound.
Don't let go the MIRACLE of PATIENCE as kind you
could be
It does not come by lending money or paying some fee.

FIFTEEN TO HAVE GRATITUDE IN KITTY

An attitude for having humbleness with a heart of gold,
pockets lot of thankfulness in its each hidden fold.
It knows one thing that others can never think more, it
holds lot of patience on its lovely shore.
Keeps on refreshing the pages of loving and living , has
for sure the heart of kindness and forgiving.
This is the ultimate test of the pebble to crackle, fifteen is
the call do you still not believe in MIRACLE.

Where does this pebble one looses for the first time , it is
probably; when one delivers someone's mime.
Giving the credit for someone work on field, is the
moment when gratitude to be given was pure need.
However sidelining the one who actually was prime, is
sure a story where you as villan committed crime.
Though it sounds like a casual moment to think, you
could have given this thought a little caring ink.

Kindness gives you a platform to stay humble, surely
it helps you alert in situational cookie crumble.
One can bulldoze the feelings whatsoever and repeat,
one can break the the golden heart to miss the beat.
The one who is not encouraged and given the real due,
will loose the trust in such more moments few.
It will pass fly every time when one makes it repeat,
lower gets the worth and slower the energy seat.

The habit of gratitude is to be practiced best, ask the tiny
little birds feeding their young's in the nest
Every time the little birdy gets fed by worm through the
beak, chirp chirp says it with gratitude every week.
The mother bird gets encouraged to feed them more, that
is nature showing thankfulness galore.
The cycle continues and bird gets ready for flight, he is
all up beat to conquer the sky with might.

The birdy little once takes the sky ; never looks
back, soars up to the heavens with no energy lack.
Here he comes back looking for his tree, just in case
there is a lunch kept by mother for free.
Sooner he realizes the act of giving was a natural need,
overthinking it is ; there was nothing to heed.
There was a lesson hidden in act for sure, the MIRACLE
of giving is limit less if kept pure.

One who anticipates in return an act for an act , is for
sure a filth and a selfish soul in fact.
You need not answer a charity with a feed, you need not
react as for a friend in need is a friend indeed.
it is selfless and pure the way it was with birds, it is no
different in water or land; for animal herds.
Keeping it like a deal or a paper contract at will, makes
the gratitude lousy, greedy and surely ill.

Greed is a filth which bombs and make 'thanks' perish,
never it remains an act of integrity for life to cherish.
Ego destroys it more and coats it with sugar an salt, the
selfless journey shows signs to make it halt.
Anger brings the element of fire to it , rendering
gratitude to remain a patient in ICU 'unfit'.
It dies of its own with the time as it leads, neither it
flowers or brings life to new seeds.

One must not take the Gratitude as a gift, it is then when
your heart starts beating with selfish rift.
It takes the toll on the element of trust and pushes us for
run, the gap of understanding gives benefit none.
The MIRACLE makes it meet only in those times, when
'might you own' tunes with all pebble rhymes.
Take a pledge to thank someone today and some
tomorrow, faith brings life and feeds kindness to borrow.

SIXTEEN TO BE COMPASSIONATE

Reaching here is a milestone for surety, reading so far is
the need anticipated for purity.
There is focus one has shown for being in here, pat
yourself; set time to celebrate and cheer.
One can be compassionate if you know where to be ,
loving it and reaching for it is the only need to see
Taking it by choice is not the option one gets, taking it
more and faking it less is the oath one sets.

Let us rhyme a popular story of the past for free, it is
often remembered as "story of the giving tree".
There was a little boy a big tree apple in cast , playing
around the tree was his favorite past.
All he does was running around it and then sleeping in
shade, there was all fun and no happiness to fade.
Swinging on its branches and eating the apple fruit, tree
found it so loving; besides the boy was super cute.

Tree loved and cherished the moments the boy had
around, giggling with sounds of sleep on the ground.
The boy started growing big and plays became few ,
Gosh! the tree felt sad as no one around to crush the
dew.
One day the grown up boy returned sad as he sat down,
tree felt bad as he looked like a soiled gown.
Why don't you come often and swing on my arm, why
do not you come and make happy charm?

Hey tree I am big and cannot climb now high, as I need
money for my friends; and few toys to buy.
Take these apples and sell them in the mart, get some
money to have some toys in the kart.
The young boy was happy and he did the same, felt so
honored as giving tree was in love game.
As the young man grows big and huge, he needed to
build a place for his living refuge.

Tree gave the entire wood as he wanted the man to
cheer, this is pure love and giving was all around here.
Now the same boy grew soggy and aged very old, he
came to the same tree with the body half fold.
Looking at the old man the tree was all in charm , as he
sees his little friend was happy in his farm.
He sat down and slept at the foot of the tree, cherished
all moments to set the soul free.

WOW! this is the story we have all in books, refreshing
it is and poetic it looks.
Teaches us selflessness and care in full , 'giving is all that
counts' with love to pull.
Enduring nature of relationships even when people and
circumstances change.
Compassion is one MIRACLE which one gives more gets
more in range.

The story of giving tree resembles us and parents as tree,
love and care was all up the sleeves for free.
We felt playful and excited to be delighted in looks,
meals and funny days with no fishy books.
We utilize them all till we grow big and they grow old,
unaware of the story yet to unfold.
The compassion dies its own death as it ceases, it starts
showing the frills with no creases.

It sometimes become too late for us to act, life long the
old bones surely perish in fact.
The realization comes when the damage is done, we
actually loose we what really had to won.
All relationships and collaborations are to be dealt with
ease, life comes once and not on some lease.
MIRACLE of compassion must not be forgotten, no ones
likes things which are rotten.

Take the pledge of showing heart to heart, keep the
deeds good inside love kart.
Don't wait to deliver till someone show, don't be
buffoons' and tend to remain low.
Give it , show it, spread it it every single ride, don't keep
emotions in buckets to hide.
Do the deed as it comes and say yes to MIRACLE, it is
not a hard nut for you to CRACKLE.

SEVENTEEN FOR TRUST TO GROW

True it stands by you if you keep it near, trust is the
name of the MIRACLE; it grows here.
It is a building of the pebbles to keep one right, the more
you build ;more it grows in height.
Standing tall in all the circumstances is at its core, belief
and faith keeps it good and progressively more.
There is nothing in this world where it doesn't exist, it
would be infinite; a long- long list.

Ever been to a chemist who gives you medicine pill,
without giving a second thought we gulp it down the
hill.
There is no mark of doubt we get, there is always the
trust in the deal we set.
Infact the basic element for any deal to succeed, is this
MIRACLE the pebble of TRUST indeed.
This was the element in the story of the clever crow,
faith; trust and lot of patience in the row.

What build this element let us break it out, what makes
this element interesting , let us shout.
TRUTH is the pillar which marks its beginning, it is
never a shot played once out of a sling.
You can never twist it and turn it for your comfort ,
indeed sometime they way we speak; it gets hurt
No difference one makes if one pitches it on the wall of
lies, leaves them dead with scavenging flies.

RELAIBILITY is the second one which makes its base,
packs it in the MIRACLE ; with strong lace.
Ability is its cousin and the REALITY its friend, the truth
stays as pure till it reaches to the end.
Wondering what is new in this we all know by heart, we
have always lived it ; we are already smart.
Be truthful if you had never doubted someone known,
reliability is the virtue with no mute tone.

The third pillar which makes the trust is YOU, Truth
and reliability sandwiched in queue.
You can be the make or break link for rest of it, trust me
it cannot grow if one is not fit.
Staying humble and remaining kind, will help the trust
to stay in bind.
It lives in you and stays with you for a happy soul, deceit
and being rude; pushes it thru sink hole.

STRENGTH the fourth pillar is all hell loose , makes it
difficult to have doubt to choose.
You would be distracted to act in vain, it does gets
bullied around to set YOU in pain
This is the moment when your Reliability gets tested,
truth gets pushed and you get arrested.
For sure it is not the time to react and be in hurry,
STRENGHT is all one needs to push down worry.

Truth-Reliability-U -Strength-THANKFUL is all what
muscles it, this is powerful five ;a blockbuster hit.
Any pillar one looses to stand by your way, will set the
fire on this dry bunch of hay.
It will be charred to soot and will start dusting around,
you will loose the jug and its base camp ground.
You can win the stars if you know to keep up TRUST,
ever try to fiddle and drop the guard, it will RUST.

EIGHTEEN TO SHOW MATURITY

The number eighteen has got a significance of charm,
pebbles of MIRACLE saves you from getting harm.
It makes you strong as you become mature, it is a
milestone and a feeling so magically pure.
You are reading which means there is story a lot ,
fighting spirit and will to fight on your side you got.
It is not just a number you have on the life line, doesn't it
really mean you have grown and you are fine.

It has a scale of it own when you are gauged, it is a
virtue to remain calm; when you are raged.
Shouting on someone to think you made your pose, you
are thorning someone and acting like a rose.
The calmness in your in stance is the other side
expecting, you break loose by simply reacting.
Growing is the process so one must not hop, MATURITY
is when you know how to put full stop.

The story of "golden touch" is something which i can
relate, how a king brought down his own fate.
Midas had a kingdom with a lot to cheer, he was in awe
love for his beautiful daughter dear.
Was very kind and was known for his deeds, was always
on the life for giving seeds.
The people were happy and supported him a lot, he had
no enemies for his kingdom to fought.

One day while getting his deed done for a sage , he was
given a power of golden touch at such age.
Warned for the virtue it can nourish, it was greed in
pocket to make life perish.
Midas was happy as whatever it touched it turned gold,
he was unknown for the future in fold.
Started small as he touched things and made people
happy, greed was yet to hit to make things peppy.

Maturity was to reject the wish given by saint, life for
him would have great story to paint.
He was doing anyway all the things with deed, love and
sharing for family kingdom to feed.
Anyways now with the power he hold, even the food
he tried touching was turning gold.
He cried as he could not touch anyone he love, the greed
of power made sobbed him in full now.

Looking at the father the princess cried, she was
unhappy for he could have taken other side.
Could not control the crying eyes her father had, story
which was great; turned by greed so bad.
She ran to the arms of his father to console him,
Whoosh! the princess turned to gold till rim.
This was the story for greed to show you understand,
situations would come and go for maturity to land.

Be vigilant when you are on the brim of chapter
eighteen, greed and ego would be flying on scene.
You would have to be aware for the self you get , need to
take care for surroundings and situations to set.
MATURITY is miracle which does not come by age, it
would come by choices you make in life-box cage.
Learning it at the cost of your own experience is must,
remember to sail well in sunny, storm or windy gust.

NINETEEN TO LOOK AHEAD

It all depends on which side of the life you look, after all
one is the master of its own life book.
All the eighteen chapters you just read and took the
travel, was sand sometimes and sometimes gravel.
It makes one to understand to look ahead, past being
good or bad; present needs to be well said!
One can have life in bloom for present to store, keep the
PEBBLES of MIRACLE at your core.

Drawing my inspiration from the thirsty clever crow,
looking ahead was all in its visionary brow.
The jug was just the task for any crew to make, honesty
and perseverance was all there with nothing to fake.
Pebble by pebble he made the water to come up ,
quenching the thirst was the winning cup.
Small and big pebbles he took ;for few he gave a drop, he
knew exactly when to look ahead and when to chop.

Looking ironically if eyes were not on head, the idiom
'looking Ahead ' would have been differently said.
We would have started by saying Look ATAIL, as there is
eye on foot and definite head to fail.
Brain would have been wired so long to act, as eyes
would have been on foot in fact.
The sensory system we all own would have a story
different, Spoooooof! a new world with happy feet on
rent.

Not looking ahead would have been a song, as eyes on
the foot would have seen no wrong.
Brain would have some shut time to think, as eyes on the
foot would take some time to wink.
One would have considered the foot as guide, eyes
as mentor and network so wide.
Crying expressions would been all so fun, with eyes
leaking on foot and slippery boots to run.

The world we all live in has lot of meaning, it does need
some brushing and some cleaning.
After all the senses you got have one common aim, they
want their master with no action lame.
The coordination they bring is a puzzle by thought, no
mater what! they will stay to order and sort.
what they give us is the ultimate gift of love, Now i
wonder why to say LOOK AHEAD for now.

The expression for Eyes can hear and ears can see, has
got to do something for me!
Eyes can hear interpret the visual cues it picks,
understanding situations with observatory flicks.
It means to interpret the body language it behold, it
means to understand the intent the situation sold.
So by all means looking ahead does make sense, it is
always to live in present and not in past tense.

Ears can see interpret the auditory cues it picks,
understanding surrounding with listening flicks.
It means to interpret what it listens to make things
feel, senses on the head and ways to seal.
It can interpret the tone of a voice, what is behind
someone's words by its noise.
So rightly putting to rest the idiom looking ahead, all
supported by your senses; well said!

This brings us at the end of chapter nineteen, with lots of
lesson to learn and filth to wash and clean.
Being you own master is all up in the kitty, reading
through chapters resounds you are witty.
The values we all have lived with and grown, can be re-
soiled ; watered and sown.
Fill your lungs with deep energy and thoughtful oxy
puff, simple can be a life ;don't tend to be rough.

TWENTY TO SUCCESS

By all means in the world of sadness and sorrow, there is
always one element the time we need to borrow.
It has the cure for everything it touches in fame, it is no
different for anyone; as it is all same.
All it needs the pebble of patience which the crow
already had, there is no need to be worry some or to be
sad.
Each sunset is followed by the sunrise and a morning
beauty, staying and trying whatsoever is your duty.

Someone says that easily got is easily lost, and few says
hardly got is hardly lost!
There is no shot put or a long javelin throw, trying it
every time sets it closer in the row.
Success is neither a stop nor a destination, it is a failure
died with lease of incarnation.
You need to keep this value on its best feeds, don't stop
at one till you sprout your wishful seeds.

Now let us take a deep dive in a story of school primary,
where success was taught with moral to carry.
Once there was a owl living on the OAK tree, happy he
was; living in his world care free.
He used to observe and listen to the world around him,
the story was brewing in his little village rim.
He used to get sad and giggle sometime with laughter,
listening was all he doing before dawn and after.

One day he saw a little boy helping an old man, he tried
with all his strength he can.
The old man was happy by the support he got, it was the
success surely for the work he thought.
The little boy was feeling proud for what he did, this was
surely a form for his success as kid.
WOW! said the owl, now I wonder what is success, it is
pride, need not be big, scale can be less.

The other day he saw a little daughters shouting at the
mother, made him sad and aloof quieter.
With passage of time he became more sad as success was
a miss, callous he became till he head a light hiss.
He started questioning himself why doesn't it show up ,
why does success is never driven self for a cup.
With a sigh of relief the next day, he saw a farmer happy
with the grain he got and bundles of hay.

He heard of a story where the elephant jumps the fence,
sets himself out and freedom hence.
There was a person blabbering in quiet, was fighting
with self and not looking right.
Admitting that he is sad and never made any mistake,
truthful was he or was he really fake.
There were others who were saying it is OKAY it came,
seasons and weather exist, don't give an excuse lame.

In his life the OWL living on the OAK tree saw a lot,
some was purely cold and some was truly hot.
There were people who changed from good to bad,
GOSH! success becomes sick and outputs become sad.
Few were those who changed for good , kindness and
faith in hand with humbleness under hood.
Some were moved from bad to worse, success was
indeed an act for curse

By observing other people the OWL became wise , this
was shear intelligence on the sunrise.
Brings me to to share the moral of the story short ,
success is all given if one observes life a lot.
You are successful when success you have is carved
out, only when it is worked and is starved out.
The MIRACLE of success is surely your might, it is you
and for your own self as per your sight.

TWENTY WON FOR PEACE

What sets one free from the clutches of time , is the
LEAP OF **FAITH** in melody of Rhyme
It the first pebble the crow was encouraged to
take, lesson we must not have just for the sake.
Element which one makes thing to bind well, is this
miracle of **KINDNESS** to blind the hell.
It was the second pebble the crow took, he knew that it
deserves the pick as shining it look

Element which does all the talking when you need
to admire, is the touch of **LOVE** you need to fire
Hot as rose and cold as ice, this was the third pebble
crow took looking at the water so nice.
The one which needs a patience on the peak, is the
miracle of **PERSEVRANCE** to sneak.
Crow was looking for it for a time long, fourth is the
pebble he picked with his crow song.

Element which is must to be drowned to sink, is the
power of **FILTH** to de-link.
Crow was choosy in picking this pebble five, as he
kicked it down to shut it up live.
When you are ready to defend someone's rage, here
comes the help by miracle of **COURAGE**
Our clever crow was sprung in action with pebble six to
pick , down it goes to give pebble five a kick.

Alerting is the game when to you want to play right,
bringing the miracle of being **BEACON** is a way to fight
Our thirsty crow was all set it to do a crackle, seventh
pebble to pick was indeed his miracle.
When one needs to push and never wants the list hate ,
here come the potion and a power to **MOTIVATE.**
Crow here was sure to not keep away his fate, picking
the pebble in the same order was indeed number eight.

When there is no dearth of taking responsibility in
the pocket, the miracle of **DEDICATION** flies the rocket.
The thirsty crow was quick on picking the pebble nine,
watching the water coming up as faith was fine.
Pebble tenth **HONESTY** was the need for the game ,
eleventh being **RESPECT** with no to shame.
Twelfth was the wonder of **CARE** to cure, thirteen was
the portion of **PATIENCE** so pure

HUMBLE was the pebble for being fourteen,
GRATITUDE would remain in power at fifteen.
Showing **COMPASSION** is sixteen in order,
Seventeen being the **TRUST** to stay on border.
The crows picks the pebble eighteen for being **MATURE**,
nineteen to look **AHEAD** to stay pure.
Free cheers for the pebble twenty of SUCCESS as ace ,
this is way to the pebble twenty one for **PEACE** to lace.

The **MIRACLE to CRACKLE** is the journey not to fake, it
is sure a success to set and make.
It can stay in air or can take the place to grind , ensure
this address is clear to find.
There is lot to learn being an Author so deep , promising
journey of values surely to keep
Let me put an end to this new found start, it beats with
me and **now beats in your HEART.**

www.ingramcontent.com/pod-product-compliance
Lightning Source LLC
LaVergne TN
LVHW011056200726
843509LV00011B/1421